Tips for learning together

This workbook is full of enjoyable activities to help your child practise the ~
techniques as at school. You don't need to do lots of preparation ~
that if your child is unsure about how to spell a word u~   t:

1 Ask your child to sound the word out.

2 Encourage them to write the letter or group
of letters (the grapheme) that represents each
sound (the phoneme) as they sound the
word out.

3 This will help them to realise that they know
how to spell some, most or all of the word.

~   ~ace. You don't need
~   ~ok in one sitting.

6 Finish each session on a positive note,
with a reward sticker.

Definitions of the sounds or term
being practised.

Fill the gaps and other
fun spelling activities.

Have fun!

Tips for
your child.

Collect puzzle pieces to
complete the images on
the sticker chart.

Identify common spelling
patterns in the ditties.

Collect reward
stickers.

For more information and support on spelling, punctuation and
grammar look at our website **www.oxfordowl.co.uk**.

The sound **/ai/** as in *train* can be written in different ways:

ai	**ay**	**a-e**	**a**	**eigh**	**ea**	**ey**
rain	play	lane	acorn	eight	break	they

Choose the correct letter group to complete the words.

ay	a-e	ai	ey	ea

T____k____ the c____k____ to the party.

Don't be l____t____! We'll have a gr____t time!

Write the correct words to complete the sentences.

Here is the _____!
It's yellow and grey.

The _____ has arrived.
At last we're on holiday!

Add a puzzle piece to your chart!

Tip: Make sure you have used the correct letter group for the /ai/ sound.

The sound /igh/ as in *bright* can be written in different ways:

igh	y	ie	i	i-e
kn**igh**t	dr**y**	t**ie**	f**i**nd	smi**le**

Choose the correct letter group to complete the words.

igh   i-e   i   y   ie

The moon was sh_____ning br_____tly in the dark

n_____t sk_____.

Look at the pictures. Add a noun with the same sound as the adjective to describe each picture.

striped

_____

bright

_____

wide

_____

Circle the letter groups that make the /igh/ sound.

He tried and tried but could not find the five bright stars in the sky!

Well done!

Sticker here

3

Prefix

A **prefix** is a group of letters joined to the beginning of a word to change its meaning. For example: *re* in *recapture*; *un* in *unknown*.

Draw lines to match the puzzle pieces and make new words.

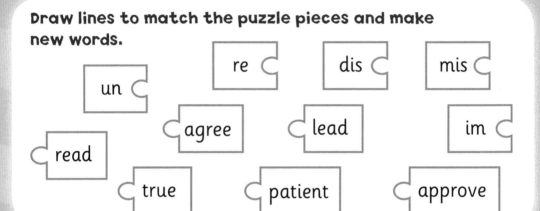

un   re   dis   mis

read   agree   lead   im

true   patient   approve

Choose the correct prefixes to complete the caption.

un   re   dis   mis   im

The gulls ____ behaved. Dad ____ likes seagulls!

Circle the prefixes • • • • • • • •

The impatient and unlucky frog misread the sign. It said 'Unfriendly crocodiles!'.

Suffix

A **suffix** is a group of letters joined to the end of a word to change its meaning.
For example: *-er* in *maker* (a person or machine which makes something);
-ness in *happiness* (the state of being happy).
Inflectional suffixes are endings that change the form of the word (plural,
tense etc.) rather than changing its meaning. For example: *-es* in *bushes* (plural);
-ed in *baked* (past tense).

Did you know?

Adding -s and -es to nouns and verbs

Usually, **-s** is added to the end of nouns to make them plural
and to the end of verbs to show the present tense. But for words
that end in **ch**, **sh**, **ss**, **x**, **z** or **zz**, you add **-es**.

Add the correct suffix to the nouns and verbs.

s   es

Floppy run____ and catch____ the ball.

The firework fizz____, buzz____ and bang____.

**Write a caption for the picture
using the past tense of 'bake'.**

____
____

Well done!

Sticker
here

5

Did you know?

Adding other suffixes

Sometimes the last letter of the word has to be dropped, changed or doubled:

- Drop the **e** before adding an ending that begins with a vowel.
- Change the **y** to **i** in words like **happiness** and **carries**.
- Double the last consonant in words like **biggest**.

Add the suffixes to the words in the grid to make new words. The first one has been done for you.

Word	Suffix	New word
fun	-y	funny
hop	-ed	
hope	-ed	
fine	-est	
wave	-ing	
worry	-ed	
skip	-ing	
baby	-es	

Circle the suffixes • • • • • • • • • •

Six cats watched five funny rabbits, hopping playfully in the bright sun.

Add a puzzle piece to your chart!

Find the words with /ee/, /igh/ and /ai/ sounds in the picture and list them in the box. Then colour in the picture!

Root words

A **root word** is a word that does not contain any prefixes or suffixes. For example: *teach* is the root word of *teaching* and *teacher*.

Draw lines to match the words containing prefixes and suffixes with their root words.

happy

playing

drive

happiness

unhappy

playful

play

driver

Complete the grid by adding the root words. The first one has been done for you.

Word	Root word
runner	*run*
balancing	
loudest	
baked	
dislike	
messiest	
unusual	

Tip: Remember that the end of the root word may have been changed when a suffix was added.

Word families

A **word family** is a group of words related to each other by grammar and meaning. For example: *word, wordy, wording, word list.* Or by meaning alone. For example: *big, large, huge, enormous.*

Draw lines to link the words in the same word families. Then circle the root word in each word family.

write   writer   sadden   creation

sad

create   writing   creative

creatively

sadness   sadly   rewrite

Now write as many words as you can think of that are in the same word family as 'act' (to perform).

Circle the words in the same family as 'care'.

The carefree kitten scampered carelessly along the carefully painted wall.

Well done!

Sticker here

The sound **/sh/** as in *ship* can be written in different ways:

sh	ch	s	ti	ci	ssi
shape	**ch**ef	**s**ure	ac**ti**on	pre**ci**ous	pa**ssi**on

Add the correct letter groups to complete each sentence.

sh	ch	s	ti	ci	ssi

The cake at the birthday celebra_____on

was deli_____ous!

Floppy was on a spe_____al mi_____on.

Add the correct words containing the /sh/ sound to complete each sentence.

The _____ took out the _____.

Miss Green landed with her _____!

Circle the /sh/ sounds in the words.

Michelle the musician had a passion for sugary sherbet lemons!

Add a puzzle piece to your chart!

Syllables

A **syllable** is a word or part of a word that contains one vowel sound when you say it. For example: *vow-el* (vowel), *con-son-ant* (consonant).

Say these words aloud and underline each syllable as you say it.

fair

popcorn

handbag

rocket

carousel

running

helter-skelter

Count the number of syllables in these words and write the number beside each one.

exaggerate ☆

September ☆

Kipper ☆

direction ☆

shine ☆

artificial ☆

shell ☆

machine ☆

Sticker here

Well done!

Tip: You can exaggerate the syllables in a word to help you spell it.

The sound **/ee/** as in *tree* can be written in different ways:

ee	**y**	**ea**	**e**	**e-e**	**ey**	**ie**
bee	happy	beach	me	athlete	donkey	shield

Choose the correct letter groups to complete the captions.

| e | ee | ie | ey | e-e | ea | y |

Dad didn't s _____ the th _____ f!

Everyone had ice cr _____ ms

on the b _____ ch.

Write as many words as you can think of with the /ee/ sound.

The sound /oa/ as in *boat* can be written in different ways:

oa	ow	o	o-e	ough	oe	eau
road	snow	old	stone	dough	toe	gateau

Circle all the words with the /oa/ sound.

There was snow on the road, so the man took the sled. He fastened the boy on with rope, and told the dogs to go!

Add the correct words with the /oa/ sound to complete the caption.

Floppy took the _____

even _____

it belonged to Joe!

Homophones

A **homophone** is a word which sounds the same as another word but has a different meaning and usually a different spelling. For example: Dad made the cake with *flour*. / Mum put a *flower* in the vase.

Draw lines to match the homophones.

reed

plain

side

read

hare

sighed   hair

plane

Circle the correct homophones to complete the sentences.

The **son** / **sun** is shining brightly.

Floppy is running **to** / **two** the **see** / **sea**.

The windsurfer's **sail** / **sale** is white and yellow.

Circle the homophones

I wonder whether I'll get a medal if I meddle with the weather!

Add a puzzle piece to your chart!

Circle the correct homophones to complete the captions.

"Oh **no** / **know**!" cried Dad. "We've got wet **feat** / **feet** but no fish."

"Where **would** / **wood** the **dear** / **deer** go if Pudding **Would** / **Wood** couldn't be saved?" asked Craig.

Draw lines to match the homophones to the correct pictures.

pair

pear

8

beach

eight

ate

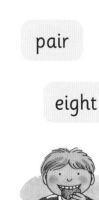

beech

Well done!

Sticker here

Silly ditties

Add in the missing words to complete the silly ditties. The missing words have the same sound as the word that is underlined in each sentence.

| play | boat | coat | knight |

The <u>bright</u> child said to the _____ ,

'Don't slay the dragon <u>today</u>.

Let's _____ !'

The <u>toad</u> in a _____

showed the <u>goat</u> in a _____

where to go.

Now think of your own word to complete the ditty.

Floppy was really muddy.

He was <u>happy</u> but <u>very</u>

_____ !

Well done!

Sticker here